RELIQUARY BESTIARY

poems & archives

MITALI KHANNA SHARMA

Published by Black Sunflowers Poetry Press
www.blacksunflowerspoetry.com

© Mitali Khanna Sharma 2024

ISBN: 978-1-7396267-7-8

All rights reserved

for the kin of the borderlands

from Punjab to Palestine

CONTENTS

1. Foreword
2. The Naming
3. Inventory at the Borderlands
4. The Only Thing Between Me & Him
7. Prolonged Grief Disorder
9. Ghazal for Valley Girl
11. Elegy for Tomorrow
12. Inventory at the Amritsar House
13. Cenzoic Strata #081547 – #081522
15. Red Eye, This Nazar
17. Ghazal for Ghazals
19. A Vessel is a Thing with Limbs
22. No Sky, Just Sex
23. Reliquary Bestiary
24. Prostration

25. Notes & Acknowledgements

Foreword

I never thought I'd think so much about belief. But I think so much about bone & blood and all that bone & blood dries into is a relic of genealogy. Each atom of mine is so heavy, so bent by its longing: for God, for many big & little gods, for a land that mourns and erupts into delight beside it. For instance, my friend noted that we all gravitate to Spain because we are all held in little cells in Spain. We can stare at the wailing virgin & her dead son beneath some medieval archway and wail ourselves because, somehow, our blood is also there. Our blood, our songs, of elsewhere are also there. And so it remains, enchanting us —

The Naming

this, a catalog of spaces

      not-poets   not-madmen

         some poets

                          some madmen

when I think of the 19th century, I become hysteric

                          and so watery

when I think of the darkest ages, I lose myself in God

                          and sinews

when I cave, I prophet

                          so sick

          of unity

      and liberty

I want a clay room with green rugs

         and a bronze kettle and a

                        salamander friend.

I want a prayer room,   named

      with windows and curtains

Inventory at the Borderlands

staggering deer
one of my kin
folk of the poppy
fields like flooding
covers, enough for two (or more)
bones, enough for us to hold
ourselves, for protecting
the remaining apostle
fallows, needing tending
the moving of the precious metal
music, for our own
idolatry, for our own
microbes, for our own
skin, for greeting
our own, with presents
enough to give to God,
a pendulum
            a distillery

The Only Thing Between Me & Him

is a fish that I eat, so proud of flesh
between me & my teeth,
somewhat like saying your name,
somewhat like turnips but also
somewhat not like turnips,
which have such full bodies
& such hard limbs.

I can count all the limbs
between me & the fish:
animalia, chordata,
and the spine-full
vertebrata. I can see
these like ribs or trees
or machetes, meant
(as our maker meant)
for marking time &
harvesting bondage.
& nobody will burn me
for putting all of this
(living, sacred, & still
scarred) inside my mouth,
at least not here.

The first story I heard here
was about fish & an
emperor & then one
about a palm leaf fan
& an emperor &
then one about a cow
& an emperor &
then one about snakes
& an emperor &
all this, too, via song
& silk, some meant
(as the emperor meant)
for the capital, some still
in the forms of moths.

Today, all the fish are a matter
between me & my god
they are wanderers, of oceans
of graveyards, of narcotics.
they are desert christians,
beaten by roman police &
united by a dead sea,
one meant for floating.

& the only other thing
floating between me & him
is an ocean, full of fish:
bony, jawless, & cartilaginous,
as if those were kingdoms
for the taking & for the naming
of soldiers, of djinn,
of so many reasons to
prostrate before nation & chant
flay, brother, flay,
how else might we banish
this pale pink wanting?

Prolonged Grief Disorder

If they ask:
I sweat my history like my faith, cloaked
saints in strange forms
they cross, they rood, they clay their pots
across forever —

(They are always naming these boats of kin).

There is so much God
And I am so tired.
I breathe in so many hollowed (or is it hallowed?) places
       Trees, minarets, hoods of saints, the abdomen of the moth,
       Saint Louis, Missouri, & its big canoes
And I am so tired.
And after the vaccine, my arms were so tired.
And when our daughter cries, I will be so tired.
There are so many histories, so many strange forms
I fill in the night.

And if they ask:
in your arms, I can be so tired and still
fed by the anointing:
your humpbacked song, your body of the veil,

the moths, the worms, & the left

breast,

swollen, resting, and feeding, still:

Ghazal for Valley Girl

We wanted this flat here. To point out that range ▲▲▲ is a sideways measure just like

words & sometimes weeping, as they spread, & cancer, until it hits skin as a cusp like

when each body ▲▲▲ in the way, like the firefly emerging on that very solstice night &

your dream of corals ▲▲▲ blessing plankton before killing them, begins to align just like

stars & moons & heavy metals ▲▲▲ are dotted & crossed & marked in time. See, what

I'm trying to say is that you make sense, being born to this web of mutation & rust like

museum jars, ethnopaleobotanical archaeology, drought, & Vitamin C gummies. It makes

so much sense that your sun is in Cancer ▲▲▲ & your mother can't remember the rest like

what second you crowned ▲▲▲ so sharp & whether the sky was black. Myth has to be the

mother of evolution. I can only imagine that's how we came so far & wide, obsessed like our own chromosomes & their constant moving & marking: drawing shapes ▲▲▲, adding

dots to lines, & chiseling crosses like they might conjure up our next niche, some nest like

a valley ▲▲▲, maybe pink, or green, or purple (in patches ▲▲▲ & only if it flowers after

snow) & so many shapes ▲▲▲ like ferns, & rivers, & bulls, all to tether like, to dress like

& maybe even, all the while we give ourselves to sickness, to give us something to be like.

Elegy for Tomorrow

here I place sum of things mundane coiled remember pickling jar shredding leftover kameez mangos limes in pickling jars leftover wax yesterday's bath the lime tree the mango tree leftover ashes the watercolor we burnt hands folding over themselves desire to touch mango skin lime skin things turn over leftover thumbs leftover burial grounds all pickled my mind mirrors cow's gut I stay here pickling between slivers taken from last breaths leave me be here I still breathe vessel of vinegar hold me still you taste too much like tomorrow I veer

left over body heat

Inventory at the Amritsar House

a blood orange

light slipping in

illuminating dust

bins filled with the leftover

ashes, some used for praying

beads, some used for praying

rugs, some used for bending

hard-necked garlic, still to slice

oranges, did I already mention

the same knife, used for cutting

hairs and nails, some cut

some cross because the nails are not clean

enough for sharing

god, enough for sharing

skin, enough for making

more, to come in

three of them, sleeping hot on the bed

Cenozoic Strata #081547 – #081522

if you emerged in the sea of this cell, then you, too, are bound by this ¹خون
& if the beast will shed, then the rest will gather their scattered cells to hold this खून²
& if there comes a little one, then there comes both big & little cells, big & little ³خون
& if we hope to conserve the crow, then we hope to conserve this खून⁴
& if the crow learns to wail, *beloved! beloved!* then it has become familiar to this ⁵خون
& if its egg seeks asylum, then its egg slips past the border through this खून⁶
& if its wail seeks asylum, then its wail slips past the border through this ⁷خون
& if I see god, then I see this खून⁸
& if I, sea of gods, then I, sea of this ⁹خون
  ∴ there is more than desolation in this खून¹⁰
  ∴ there is more than desolation in this ¹¹خون
  ∴ there is more than desolation in this blood¹²

---

[1] blood[13]
[2] blood[14]
[3] blood[15]
[4] blood[16]
[5] blood[17]
[6] blood[18]
[7] blood[19]
[8] blood[20]
[9] blood[21]
[10] blood[22]
[11] blood[23]
[12] blood[24]

[13] My great-grandfather was a godly man with a godly body
[14] meaning he had the name of god stabbed into his wrist (proximal to the cephalic vein)
[15] meaning he devoted each movement of limbs to scratching the names of gods (from right to left)
[16] meaning he was an engineer, tasked with guiding the rest over the five waters
[17] (so that no beloved would deliver their corpse to their beloved again).
[18] And despite his faith, his limbs, so many bodies did those beloveds deliver. It makes no sense.
[19] Perhaps I have too much faith in blood. I do have a watery body after all —
[20] according to what we might see in the nights:
[21] these pockets of air,
[22] part breath, those that have so proclaimed:
[23] I shall never meet the land
[24] that delivered his beloved to him.

Red Eye, This Nazar

In the old red days, when fruit was fruit
the women were said to believe in this
space, all curved & scapular, between
an arm & an arm

as an alien boat, a star-borne raft,
woven and still, one that slips and
causes slippage of other similarly
curved things: like joints, like drinks,
like departures & arrivals

but today, my women are so scared
of space & flight. All I have
known of airports have been red
visions of God & fury & missing
familiar bodies & a dream, where
you are running so scared, so
celled, and you suddenly slip
and your leg jolts, lifting the seat
of the passenger ahead of you,
his eyes locked onto the flight map.
And still, there is a sense of a creation
tale, a way to move towards

where it all fell from:
a tether.

The rolling beltway, it is full
of things & worn belongings.
It feels so close to reason,
a crashing of knowings:
a body collapsed via a body
collapsing. A body tethered via
a body in flight. And still, all these bodies
held together by nothing more than a sliver
of space.

One day, my women will stare at this spinning
from the outer space. We will see the sun in the
West and wail, *who told us to go
so far?*

Ghazal for Ghazals

This is not a nature poem. This is a blueing lip, a departed wailing song
for a sky that opened in drones and a people who began, welding song

and coal and ashes and wheat. It feels almost Midwestern, almost homely,
to trace the buried and pyred beneath such fog. Or so goes the Dylan song.

Would you believe I'm growing things here? In this radio space? It's all organic –
parsley, sage, rosemary, and all sorts of other masses. All the while pooling song.

I want to do it all with blued lids: darkened by salt and winter berries and
crushed beetle wings and an alembic. I want to do it, all the while wailing song

and folding things: like hairs, strands, hands, seas, grasses, plains, over and over
their own again and again and still feeling fuller in the sense of wanting song.

See, I'm condemned to growing things. To wanting to grow so many things.
I'm dreaming of children, on my back, in this radio space, still knowing song

and harvest. I'm dreaming of a God hell-bent on leaving the Isle and the Kush
with holes and so many sounds to fill them and carve them their drinking song.

It's said – in fact, pronounced – that giants wandered down from Uzbekistan into
Pakistan simply to make home in the shape of mountains and start yodeling song

through the valleys, just as giants are known to do. I wonder how I might tell this to the kids, as they think about frightening plates, and try modeling song

and even prayer and how we might, still, here, elsewhere, keep making our homes for these times of our big, big-footed hunger that just won't stop salivating song.

A Vessel is a Thing with Limbs

It's dawned on me
(just as things dawn
so messy, yolk-like,
bloody, in a sac like
worms, like fish, like prey,
like coughs bigger than the hands
told to catch them)
that I dream of bearing
a public health hazard:

one more thing with limbs,
touching
moss-like things
because mama,
how can we not
touch moss-like things,
you said we must
pass through all this air,
this blood, this sugar,
this eruption
of delight & still
sleepiness

& the weights of them all:
lilac periwinkles
green beds
lemony sheets
all of them stained
I heard (just as one hears:
breath-like, bread-like)
that space-time bends
in the name of messiness

and it is so exciting
to be alive in this time
because don't you remember?
you asked for this,
you cried for my own body,
and there is so much I've promised
to put together for you like
bread, like beds,
like chamomile tea & antihistamines
& silly shapes like deep time

I promise I promise
the moss will love you

the deer will love you

these tectonic plates are so sharp

& touching

and they will still love you

there is no other reason

for us to keep

folding ourselves back

together, out of ebbs of

piercing & touching,

so close,

like moons

like gods

like this

No Sky, Just Sex

The eucalyptus praises itself with volatile oils.
And still, I am convinced that it praises others
and opens breath. And still, if the eucalyptus was
the end-point, God would slip his finger in here,
hoping, and still, there would be no sign, no miracle.
There would only be flame, flame without miracle.
Flame without gift. We wouldn't be able to come
to know. We wouldn't be able to tell what kind
of flame this is. We wouldn't be able to graze each
other and wonder, is this your hand or the hand of God?
We would begin to pray that the night never ended,
while beginning to untangle somewhere between
our species. The morning light would be so sharp and
pocketless. There would be no landing place between
fibers and stitches. There would be no soil, and no soiled
ones for touching and for curing. There would be no miracle.
There would be no clot to spring forth from and begin
to drink, like buffalo or gin or the headbanging of believers
and goats. There would be nothing to say about it.
No words.
        No words.
                Not even a word for arms.

Reliquary Bestiary

If I understand it correctly, medieval Catholics were just so fucking confused and comforted by the Trinity, and I do understand that correctly because I've held my own canines too. I understand correctly that there can only be God between these folds of skin, fur, sunlight, sons, fathers and ghosts. So I'm at the dog park and I find myself pronouncing the bones behind me every day. If I understand correctly, this is a space of worship because there are so many bones beneath the soil, beneath our bodies, all being spoken once more. There are so many of us, circling our companions, holding bags of shit. I meet an old Russian man there each Monday. He asks about my children each time (though I have just the pup) and tells me that they should know Punjabi. He wants to know it too so I tell him about the Qawwali but he says he cannot touch his lips to Islam. I want to tell him that I have tongued Catholicism too. I want to tell him that I will weep for my dead and fill myself with wine beside him. But I don't. I promise to bring a God-free poem next week. Is this it?

Prostration

I have come to remember you, fractured.
In the house, I mistake dust for spirits and cough.
I mistake spirits for water, and, at times, heat.
It is so peacefully warm at times,
I can submit this to you.

Notes & Acknowledgements

The epigraph quotes four female poets, medieval and modern:

> "a sage starving to death" is taken from the first line of fourteenth-century Kashmiri mystic Lal Ded's *vakh* #30, translated by Ranjit Hoskote in I Lalla, *The Poems of Lal Ded*.

> "dented objects for gathering water" is from Myung Mi Kim's *Penury*.

> "the touches of the disappearing, things" is from "Elegy" by Aracelis Girmay.

> "not as wounds but as worships" is from fourteenth-century English mystic Julian of Norwich's *Revelations of Divine Love*.

Various lines of "The Naming" utilize the language and lore surrounding the Prophet Muhammad's revelation.

The third to last line, "flay, brother, flay," of "The Only Thing Between Me & Him" is from Tishani Doshi's "They Killed Cows. I Killed Them."

"Prolonged Grief Disorder" was previously published in *Rogue Agent Journal* (Issue 95, February 2023) and *Wordgathering: A Journal of Disability Poetry and Literature* (Volume 16, Issue 4, Winter 2022).

"Ghazal for Valley Girl" initially appeared in *MAYDAY Magazine* on October 6, 2023.

"Elegy for Tomorrow" is after "Elegy" by Aracelis Girmay.

"Cenozoic Strata #081547 – #081522" recalls the Partition of India and Pakistan, often referred to as the bloodiest mass migration in human history. This piece initially appeared in the first issue of Dublin-based *Cc: Zine* on November 1, 2022.

"Ghazal for Ghazals" was inspired by the voice and songs of Radie Peat and Arooj Aftab.

"A Vessel is a Thing with Limbs" was inspired by the poetry of Dorothea Lasky.

"No Sky, Just Sex" emerged from a reading of Kaveh Akbar's "The Miracle."

"Reliquary Bestiary" first appeared in *Cobra Milk* (Issue 04, Winter/Spring 2023).

www.blacksunflowerspoetry.com

www.ingramcontent.com/pod-product-compliance
Lightning Source LLC
Chambersburg PA
CBHW040639100526
44585CB00039B/2872